BILLY JOEL

PIANO / VOCAL / GUITAR

AN INNOCENT MAN

Additional editing and transcription
by David Rosenthal

T0079213

ISBN 978-1-4803-4478-5

HAL•LEONARD®
CORPORATION
7777 W. BLUEMOUND RD. P.O. BOX 13819 MILWAUKEE, WI 53213

In Australia Contact:
Hal Leonard Australia Pty. Ltd.
4 Lentara Court
Cheltenham, Victoria, 3192 Australia
Email: ausadmin@halleonard.com.au

Visit Hal Leonard Online at
www.halleonard.com

FOREWORD

Released in the summer of 1983, *An Innocent Man* was Billy's eighth album on Columbia Records, and his fifth to be produced by Phil Ramone. While Billy's previous album, *The Nylon Curtain* (1982), was an homage to *Sgt. Pepper* and the Beatles, *An Innocent Man* celebrates Billy's pre-Beatles influences and the soul music he loved on AM radio as a kid. Writing and recording in New York City, he immersed himself in the greats of the late '50s and early '60s—Wilson Pickett, James Brown and the Famous Flames, Frankie Valli and the Four Seasons, The Drifters, and Ben E. King. It was a fun album for him to make, a joyous time in his life, and all this is captured in the spirited songs that comprise this album.

Having played keyboards in Billy Joel's band since 1993, I have become very familiar with his music. Accordingly, Billy has asked that I review the sheet music to his entire catalog of songs. As I am also a pianist, he entrusted me with the task of correcting and re-transcribing each piece, to ensure that the printed music represent his songs exactly as they were written and recorded.

The challenge with each folio in Billy's catalog is to find musical ways to combine his piano parts and vocal melodies into playable piano arrangements. First, the signature piano parts were transcribed and notated exactly as Billy played them. The vocal melodies were then transcribed and incorporated into the piano part in a way that preserves the original character of each song. All of the songs in this collection received the same astute attention to detail. The result is sheet music that is both accurate and enjoyable to play, and that remains true to the original performances.

On "Keeping the Faith," for example, the characteristic horn lines are added in wherever possible when they fall between vocal phrases. For the intro, the funky Wurlitzer electric piano part is combined with the guitar riff and the bass line into a playable piano part. Since the song fades out on the original recording, I added an optional alternate ending that is exactly how we perform it live.

On "Tell Her About It," the signature horn lines in the intro are combined with the Richard Tee piano part in the right hand, while the bass lines are covered by the left hand. Throughout the song the horn lines are included wherever possible, and, of course, the bari sax answers are there in the chorus.

The characteristic Jerry Lee Lewis-style piano stabs of "Christie Lee" are included whenever they fall in between the vocal phrases, and on "Careless Talk" the rolled piano eighths and horn hits that answer the vocal lines are added in wherever they are playable along with the melody.

While the catchiness of Billy's melodies has made for timeless pop songs, many of his melodies and chord structures are classical in the way they are constructed. An obvious example of how well these two styles fit together is in "This Night," where he creates the perfect chorus for the song by writing lyrics to the second movement of Beethoven's "Pathetique Sonata." It melds perfectly together with a doo-wop-style verse, proving that strong melodies can transcend any genre.

An Innocent Man is a fantastic collection of finely crafted pop songs. Billy and I are pleased to present the revised and now accurate sheet music to the songs from this classic album.

Enjoy,
David Rosenthal
March 2015

CONTENTS

EASY MONEY

Words and Music by
BILLY JOEL

Brisk 4

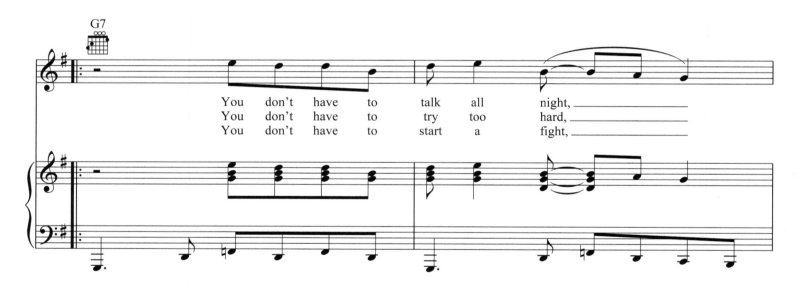

You don't have to talk all night, _____
You don't have to try too hard, _____
You don't have to start a fight, _____

I'm a man who can't say no. _____
I don't need a song and dance. _____
I'm a man who can't say no. _____

You don't have to twist my arm,
I don't need an in - vi - ta - tion,
If you've got a lit - tle risk - y bus' - ness,

just point me where you want to go. _____ Take __
if you've got a game of chance. _____ Take __
just point me where you want to go. _____ Take __

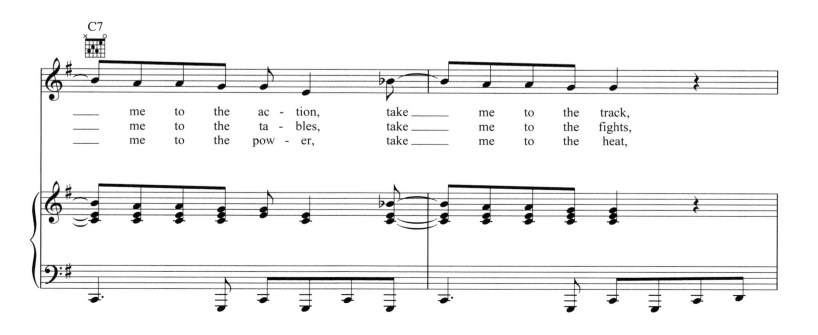

__ me to the ac - tion, take _____ me to the track,
__ me to the ta - bles, take _____ me to the fights,
__ me to the pow - er, take _____ me to the heat,

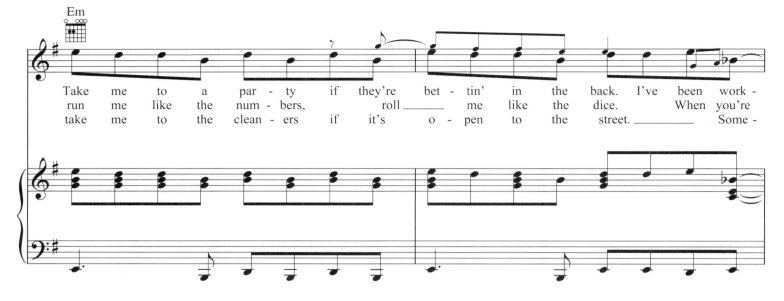

Em

Take me to a par - ty if they're bet - tin' in the back. I've been work -
run me like the num - bers, roll ___ me like the dice. When you're
take me to the clean - ers if it's o - pen to the street. ___ Some -

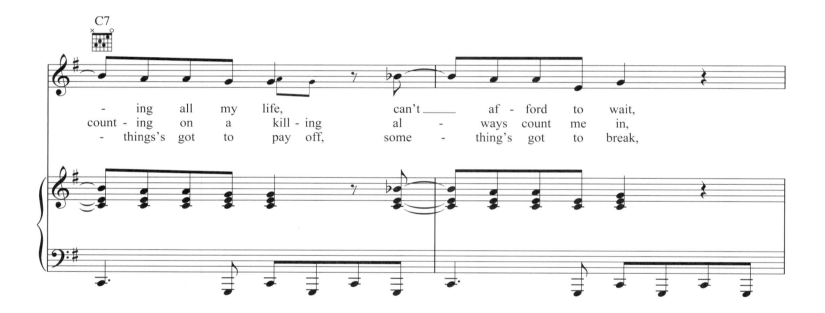

C7

- ing all my life, can't ___ af - ford to wait,
count - ing on a kill - ing al - ways count me in,
- thing's got to pay off, some - thing's got to break,

D

let me call my wife so I can tell her I'll be late. I want the
talk me in - to los - in' just as long as I can win. I want the
some - one's got a for - tune that they're beg - gin' me to take. I want the

8

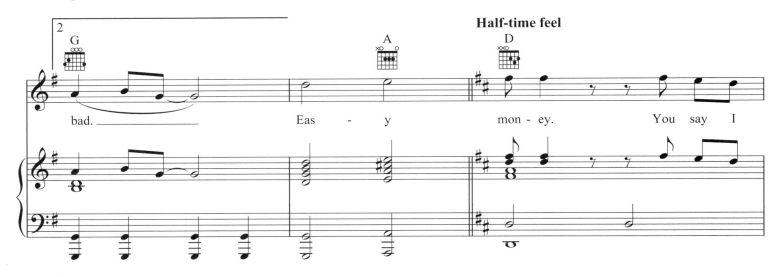

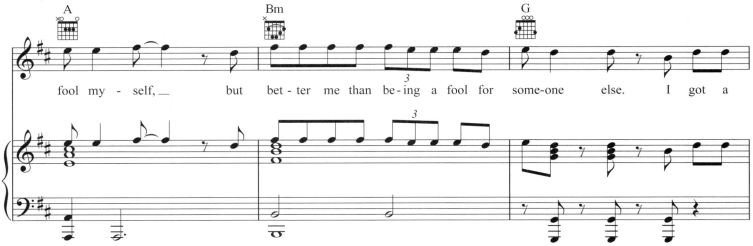

hot slot ma-chine of a sys - tem read - y to go. _____

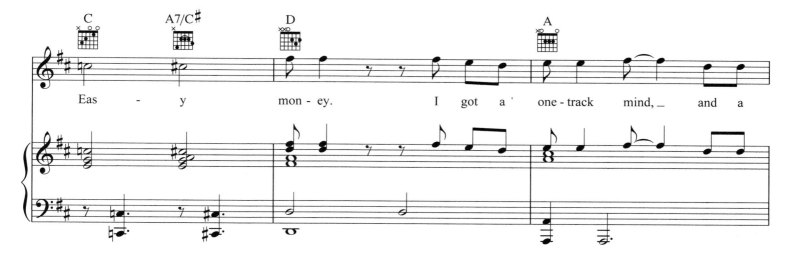

Eas - y mon - ey. I got a 'one - track mind, _ and a

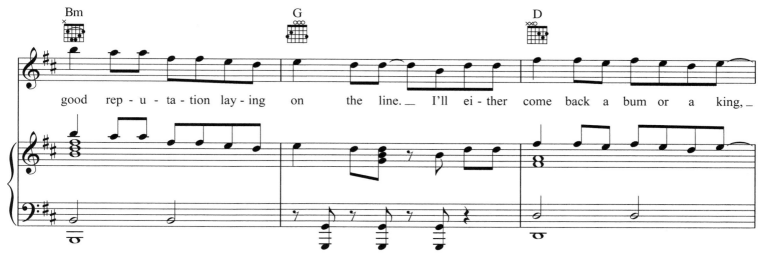

good rep - u - ta - tion lay - ing on the line. _ I'll ei - ther come back a bum or a king, _

D.S. al Coda

_ ba - by, I don't know. _____

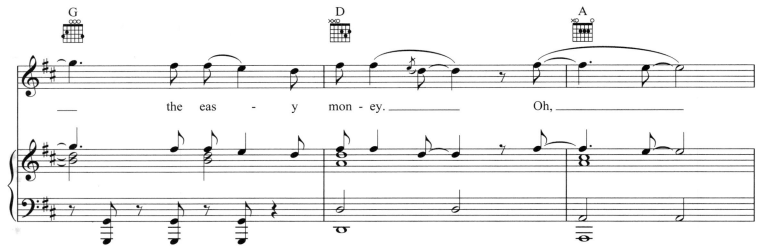

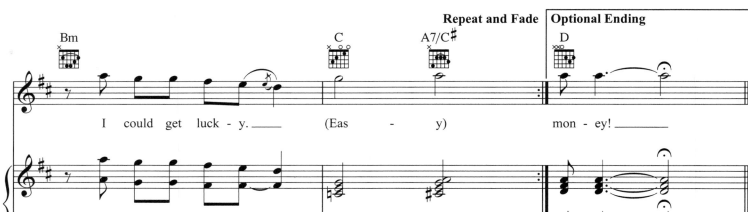

AN INNOCENT MAN

Words and Music by
BILLY JOEL

16

To Coda

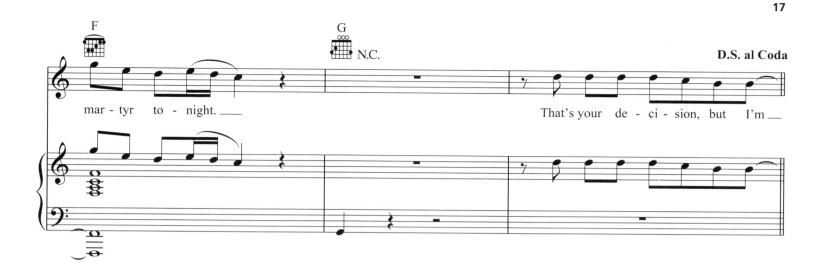

mar - tyr to - night. ___

D.S. al Coda

That's your de - ci - sion, but I'm ___

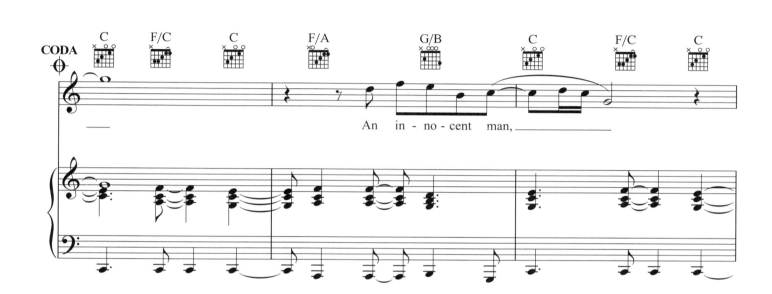

An in - no - cent man, ___

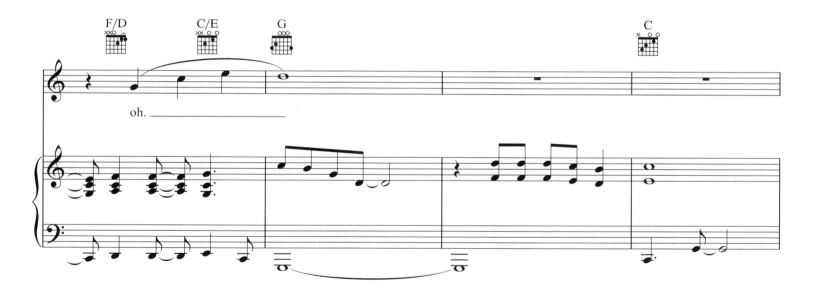

oh. ___

THE LONGEST TIME

Words and Music by
BILLY JOEL

Bright Rock and Roll

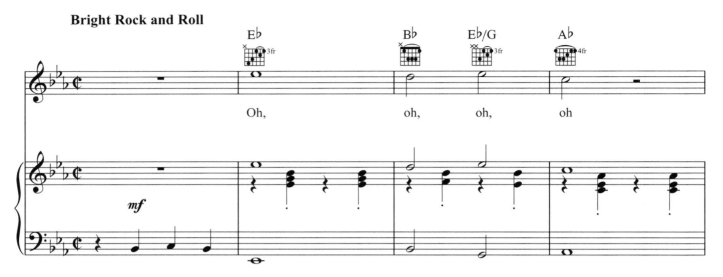

Oh,   oh,   oh,   oh

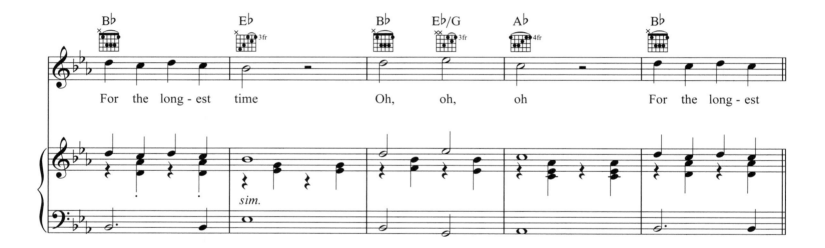

For the long-est time   Oh,   oh,   oh   For the long-est

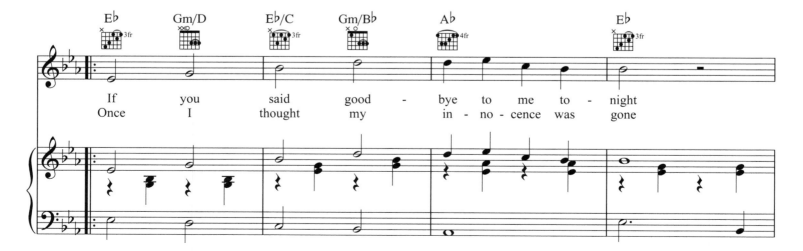

If   you   said   good - bye   to me to - night
Once   I   thought   my   in - no - cence was gone

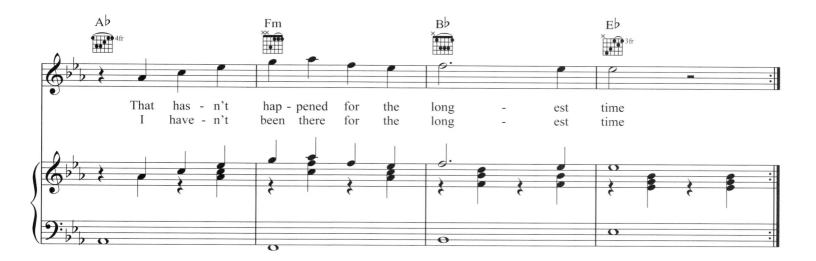

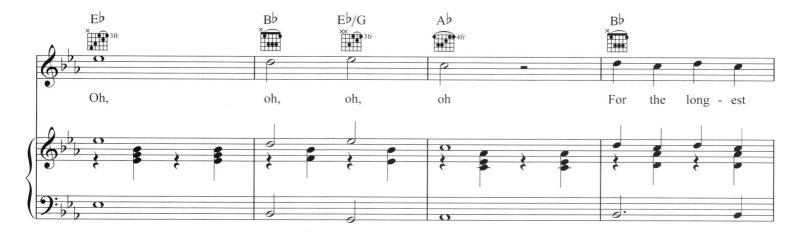

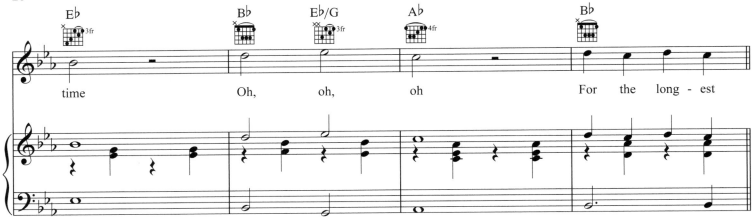

time   Oh,   oh,   oh   For the long-est

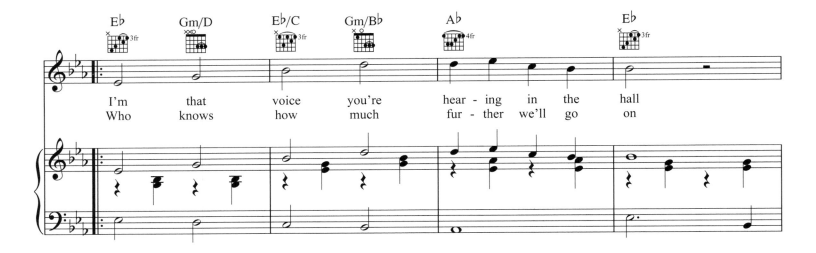

I'm   that   voice   you're   hear-ing   in   the   hall
Who   that   knows   how   much   fur-ther   we'll   go   on

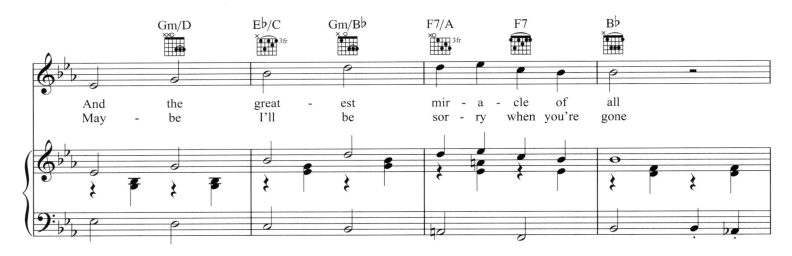

And   the   great-est   mir-a-cle   of   all
May-be   I'll   be   sor-ry   when you're   gone

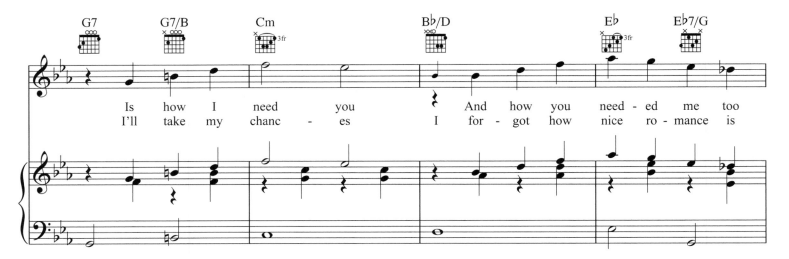

Is   how   I   need   you   And   how   you   need-ed   me   too
I'll   take   my   chanc-es   I   for-got   how   nice   ro-mance   is

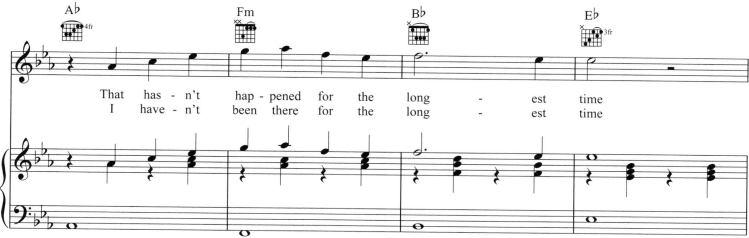

That has - n't hap - pened for the long - est time
I have - n't been there for the long - est time

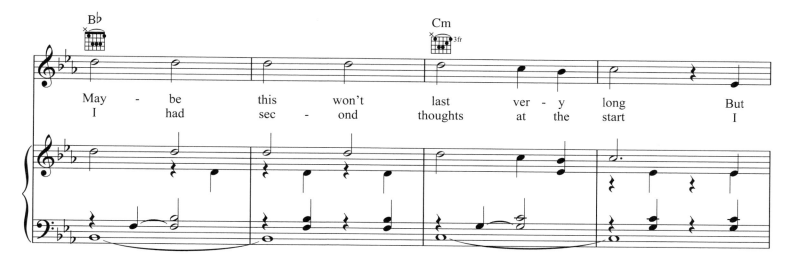

May - be this won't last ver - y long But
I had this sec - ond thoughts at the start I

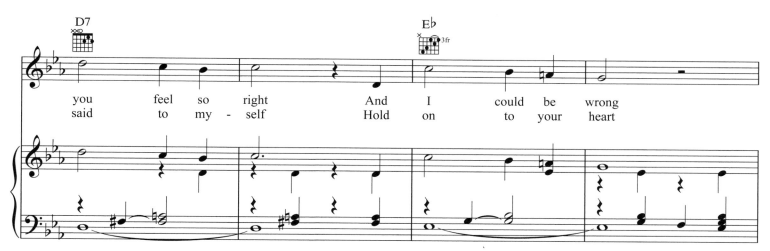

you feel so right And I could be wrong
said to my - self Hold on to your heart

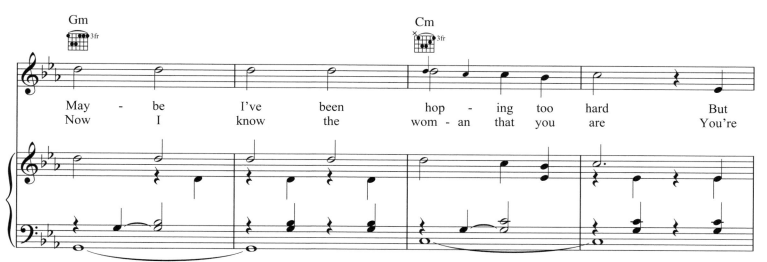

May - be I've been hop - ing too hard But
Now I know been the wom - an that you are You're

22

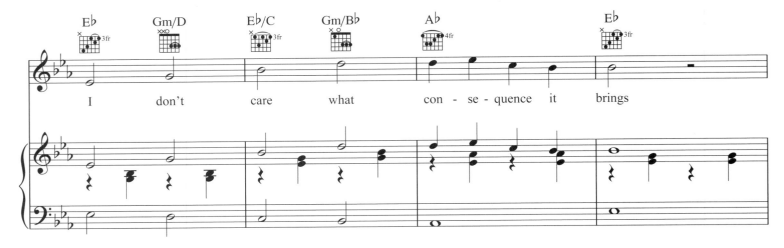

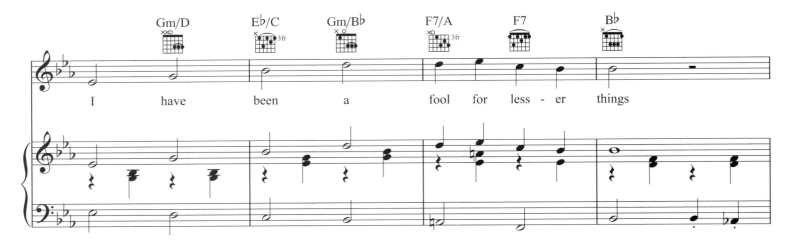

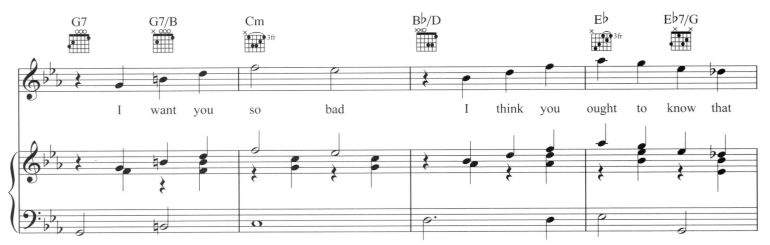

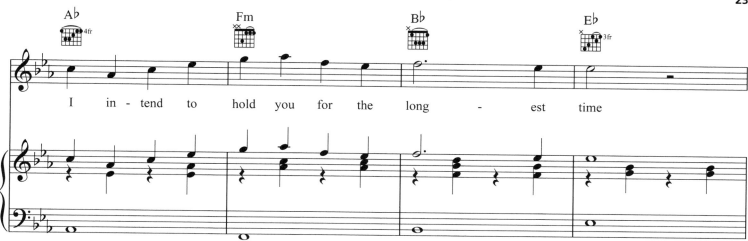

I in- tend to hold you for the long- est time

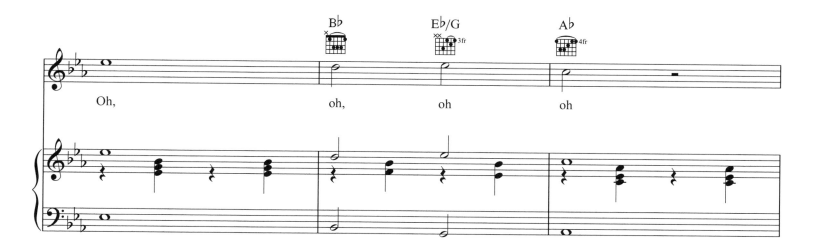

Oh, oh, oh oh

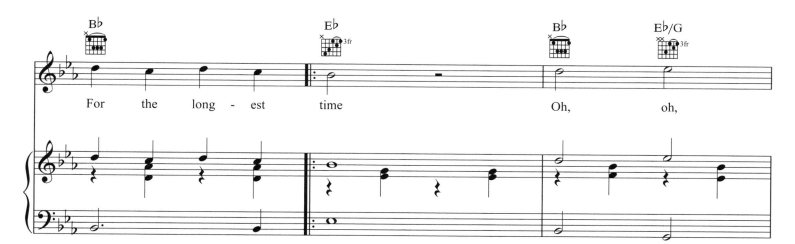

For the long- est time Oh, oh,

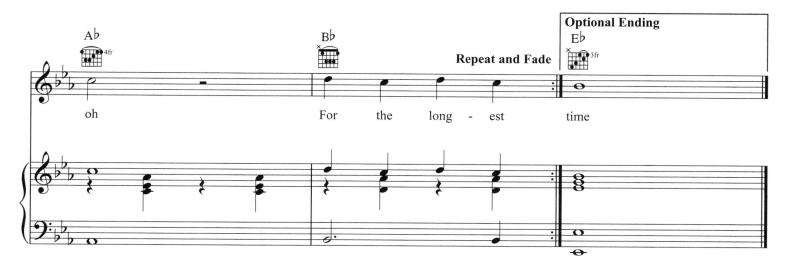

oh For the long- est time

Optional Ending

Repeat and Fade

THIS NIGHT

Words and Music by
BILLY JOEL

I start - ed break - ing my prom - is - es right there and then. _____
Are - n't you run - ning from some - one who's not o - ver you? _____

Did - n't I swear there would be no com - pli - ca - tions? _
How man - y nights have I been lone - ly with - out you? _

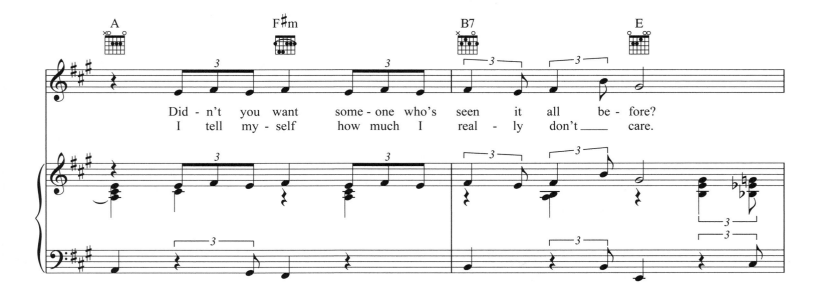

Did - n't you want some - one who's seen it all be - fore?
I tell my - self how much I real - ly don't _____ care.

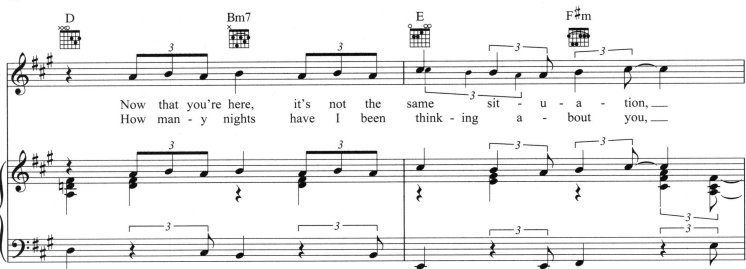

Now that you're here, it's not the same sit - u - a - tion, ___
How man - y nights have I been think - ing a - bout you, ___

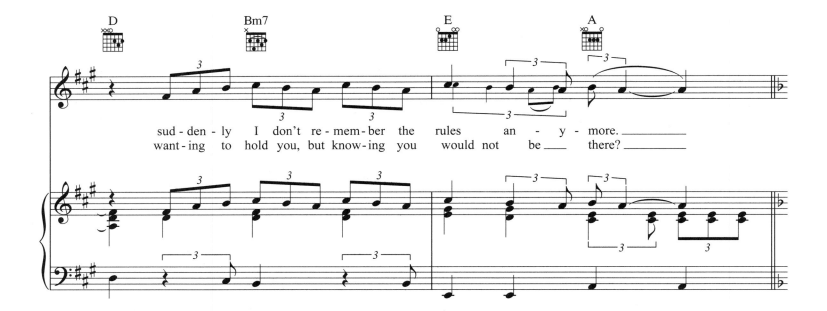

sud - den - ly I don't re - mem - ber the rules an - y - more. ___
want - ing to hold you, but know - ing you would not be ___ there? ___

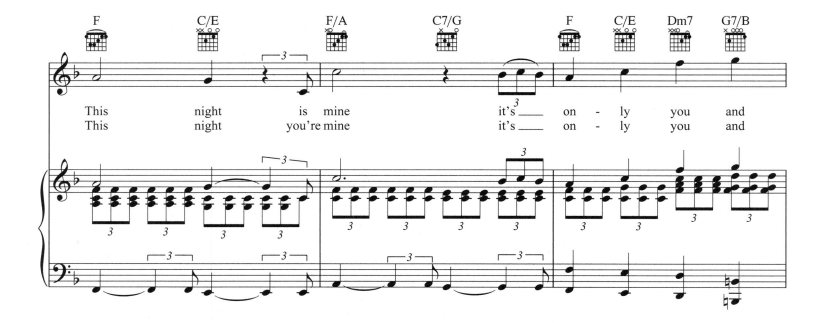

This night is mine it's ___ on - ly you and
This night you're mine it's ___ on - ly you and

I. To - mor - row _____ is a long _____ time a - way; _____
I. I'll tell you _____ to for - get _____ yes - ter - day; _____

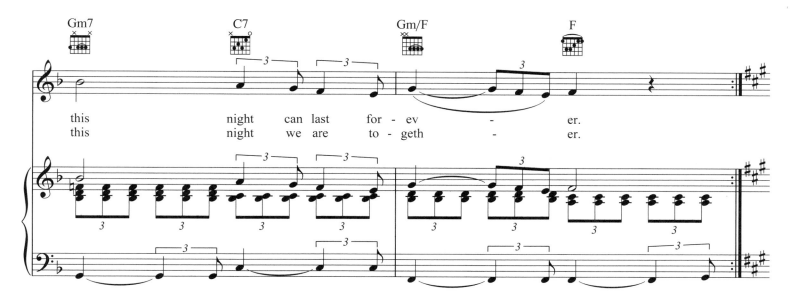

this night can last for - ev - - er.
this night we are to - geth - - er.

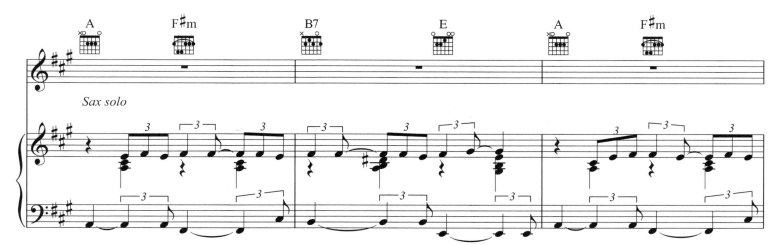

Sax solo

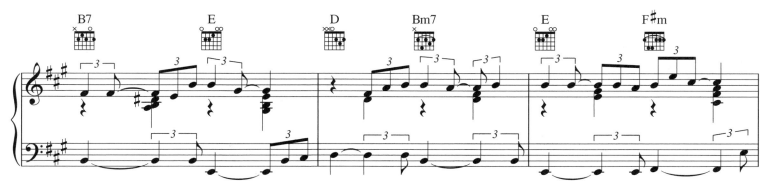

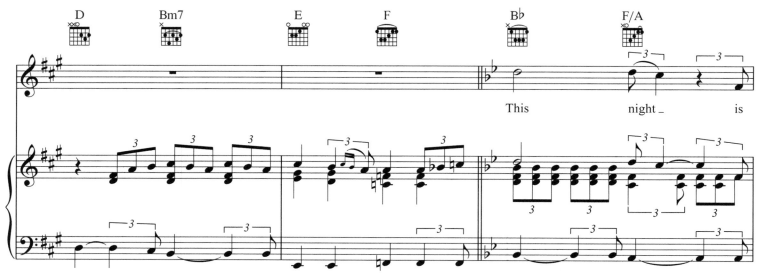

This night __ is

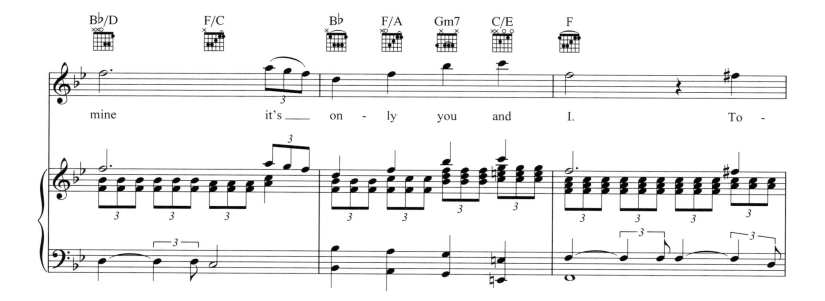

mine __ it's __ on - ly you and I. __ To -

mor - row __ is such a long __ time a - way; __ this night can last for-

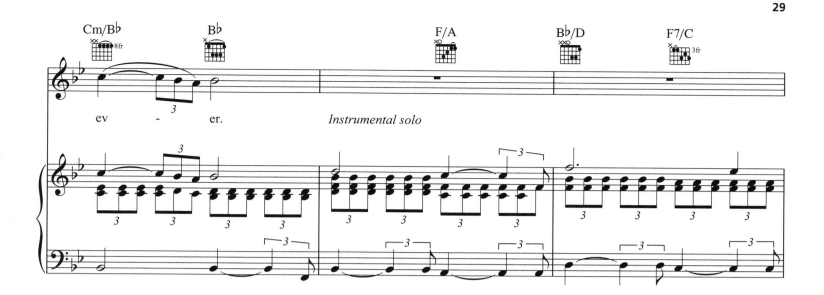

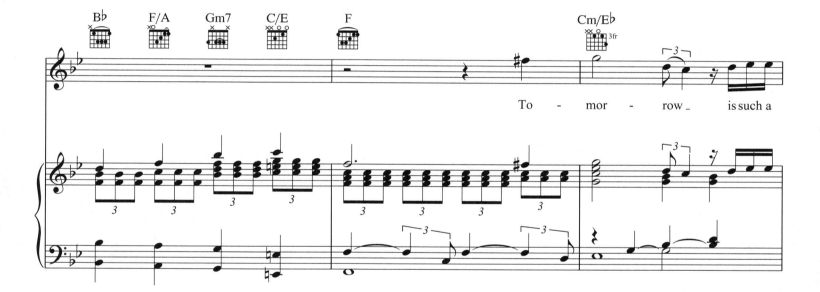

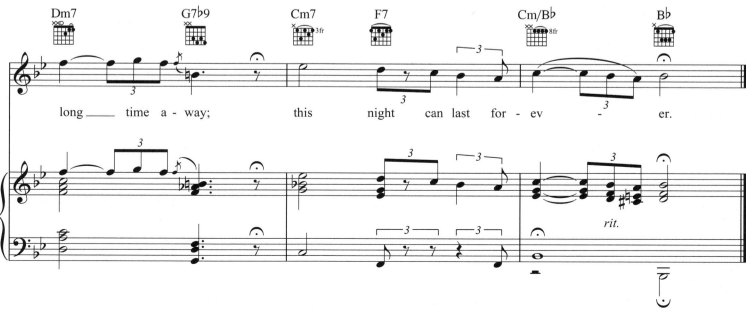

[Page 1 — track list]

Easy Money - G ↑ - harmony in bridge - 4:28
An Innocent Man - C ↓ - 5:16
Tell Her About It - B♭ ↑ - 4:24
~~Tell~~ ~~Your~~ Your Turn - D ↑
~~The Telephone~~ - E♭ →
This Night - A ↓ - 4:17
Sanctuary Song
~~Tell~~
Careless Talk - F ↑ - 4:14
Uptown Girl - E ↑ - 3:08
And So It Goes - C ↓ - 4:10 ??
Keeping the Faith - ♭ → 5:00

The Longest Time - E♭ ↓ - 3:40
Just ~~the~~ new song G
Christie Lee - C ↑
~~But~~ ~~B♭~~ Undeniably Real B♭ ↓ shuffle
Leave A Tender ~~Moment~~ Moment Alone

[Page 2 — An Innocent Man lyrics draft, heavily edited]

An Innocent Man

Some people stay far away from
the door if there's a chance of it opening up
They hear a voice in the hall outside
and hope that it just passes by
Some people
live with the fear of a touch and
the anger of having been a fool
They will never be hurt again
will tell them a lie

Don't be afraid of ~~em~~
I know you're only protecting yourself
I know you're thinking of somebody else
Someone who hurt you
But I'm not above making up for the love
That you've been denying
you could ever feel
I'm not above
anything that could
gave you some faith in a man
doing all thing if it
gives you some faith in a man
Some people
Some people
it's better to let
some people sleep alone all their
lives
Some people
say they like all the room in the bed
And maybe

[Page 3 — Tell Her About It]

Tell Her About It

Listen boy I don't want to see you let a good
thing slip away
You know I don't like watching anybody make the
same mistakes I made
She's a real nice girl and she's always there for you
But a nice girl wouldn't tell you what you should do

Listen boy I'm sure that you think you've got it
all under control
You don't want somebody telling you they way to
stay in someone's soul
You're a big boy now and you'll never let her go
But that's just the kind of thing she ought to know

Tell her about it, Tell her everything you feel
Give her every reason to accept that you're for real
Tell her about it, Tell her all your crazy dreams
Let her know you need her let her know how much she means

Listen boy, Don't take love for granted
'cause it all might fall apart
you know love can change
it won't be the same infatuation like the start
'Cause you're gonna have to like each other too
And for that to work she's got to hear from you

Listen boy it's a not automatically a certain gaurante
To insure yourself you've got to provide
communication constantly
When you love someone, you're always insecure
And there's only one good way to reassure

This Night

Didn't I say I wasn't ready for romance
Didn't I promise we would only be friends
And when we danced, though it was only a slow dance
I started breaking my promises right there + then

Didn't I ~~see~~ ~~didn't~~ ~~want~~ complications
~~Didn't we~~ ~~didn't we~~ Didn't we
Didn't I ~~swear~~ there would be no complications
~~Didn't I~~ ~~say~~ Didn't you want
someone who's been

Didn't I ~~swear~~ there would be no ~~complication~~ obligations
Didn't you ~~want~~ ~~need~~ You need someone
who's seen it all before
But now that you're here, it's not the
same situation
~~and now I'm sure~~
Suddenly I don't remember the rules
anymore

This night is more it's only ad I
Tomorrow is a long time away
This night ~~we are together~~ will last forever

How many nights when I was lonely without you
I told myself how much I really don't care
How many nights had I been ~~thinking~~ about you
wanting to hold you but knowing you would not be there
~~How many times did you believe~~
~~How many times~~
~~Didn't we say~~ ~~that we~~ only be friends

April 20-21
'83

Leave A Tender Moment Alone

Even though I'm in love
Sometimes I get so afraid
I'll say something so wrong
Just to have something to say

I know the moment isn't right
To tell the girl a comical line
To keep the conversation light
I guess I'm just frightened out of my mind

But if that's how I feel
It's the best feeling I've ever known
It's undeniably real
Leave a tender moment alone

Yes I know I'm in love
But just when I ought to relax
I put my foot in my mouth
'Cause I'm just avoiding the facts

~~When~~ If the girl ~~is~~ gets too ~~getting~~ ~~very~~ close
~~And~~ if I need ~~the~~ room to escape
When the moment arose
~~I tell her~~ I'd tell her it's all ~~this~~ ~~my~~ a mistake

~~But that's how I feel~~
But that's not how I feel
No That's not the feeling I've known
It's undeniably real
Leave a tender moment alone

Keeping the Faith

If it seems like I've been lost in ~~remember~~ Let's
If you think that means I miss my younger days
Then you should have known me much better
Because my past is something that never got in my way

Still
~~But~~ ~~I'm~~ I would not
be here now without ~~this hunger~~ If I never had the hunger
And I'm not ashamed to say ~~the~~ ~~we were~~ 'friends
~~Cause I~~ ~~the music~~
'Til I heard them ~~cause I was growing up~~
~~cause~~ ~~cause I was losing my desire~~
until ~~there was the music~~
Cause I ~~never~~ ~~would~~ felt the desire
Til their music set me on fire
Then I was saved ~~and~~ that's why
I'm keeping the faith yes I'm
Keeping the faith

We wore matador boots only Flagg Brothers
had them with a cuban heel
And Iradescent sacks with the same color
shirt with a tight pair of chinos
A sharkskin jacket with a velvet collar
In a diddy-bop grey

Bought a new pack of Luckies
and a thing called Sen-Sen
Took ~~stole~~ my old man's Trojans
and his ~~old~~ old spice after shave
Had the ~~same~~ same shiny pompadour
As the rest of the romeos are

TELL HER ABOUT IT

Words and Music by
BILLY JOEL

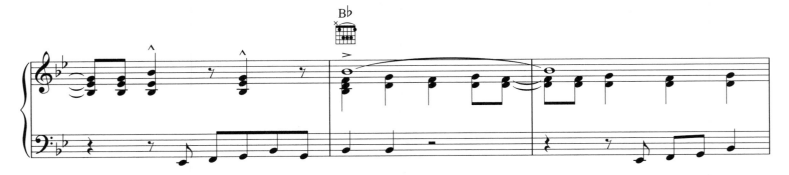

Lis- ten boy, don't _

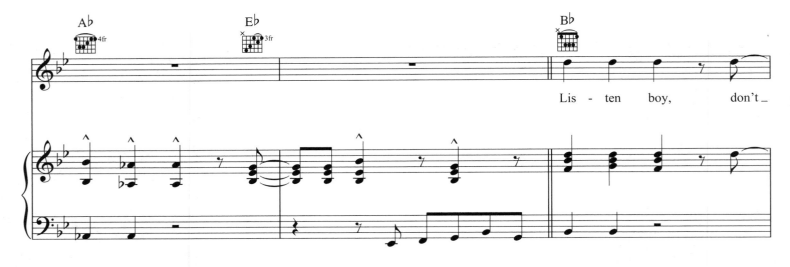

_ want to see you let a good thing slip a -way. _ You know I

don't like watch-ing an - y-bod-y make the same ___ mis-takes ___ I ___ made. ___

___ She's a real ___ nice girl ___ and she's al - ways there for you, ___

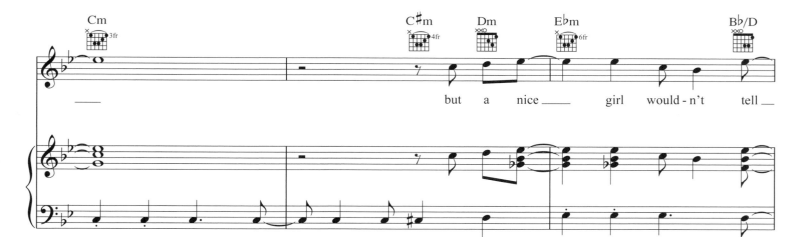

___ but a nice ___ girl would-n't tell ___

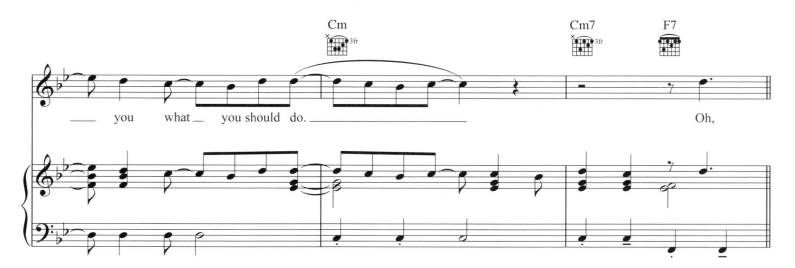

___ you what ___ you should do. _____ Oh,

Alternate melody sung 2nd and 3rd time.

your cra - zy dreams. _____
be - fore _____ you leave. _____

Let her know _____ you need _____
Pay her some at - ten -

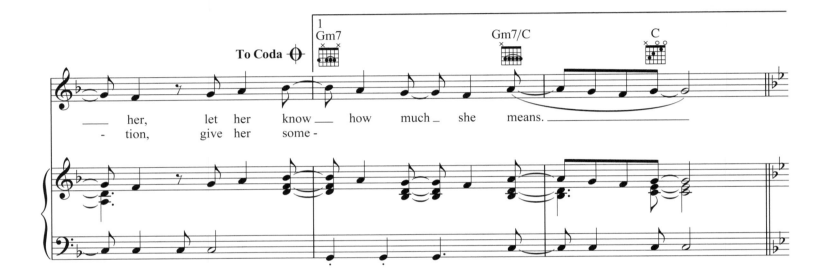

_____ her, let her know _____ how much _____ she means. _____
- tion, give her some -

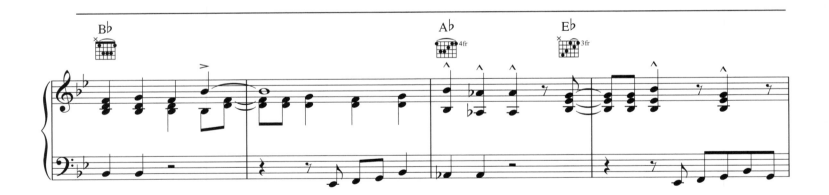

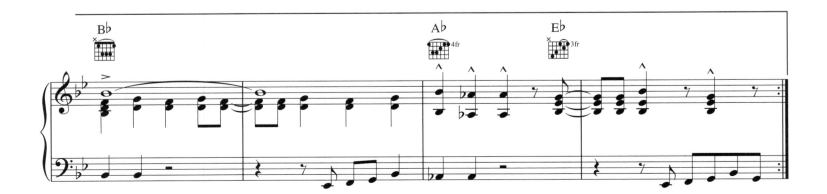

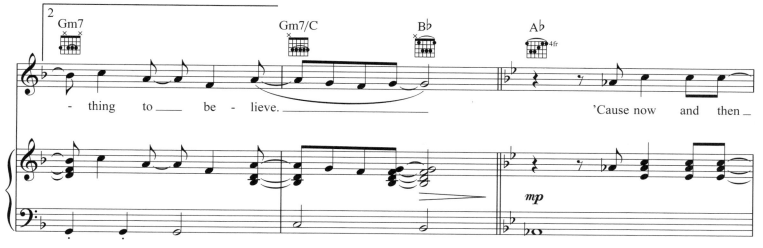

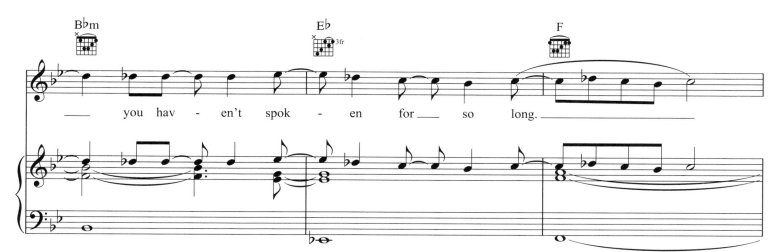

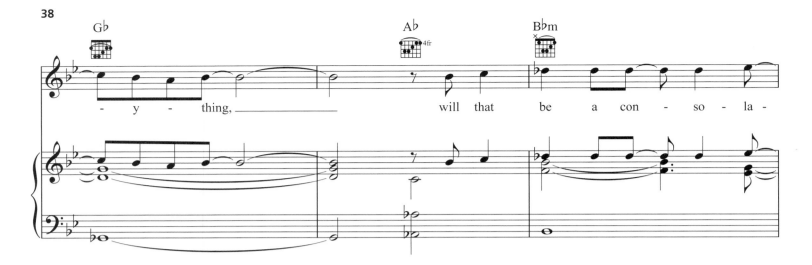

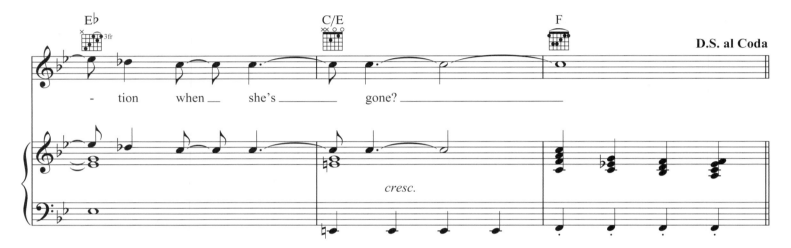

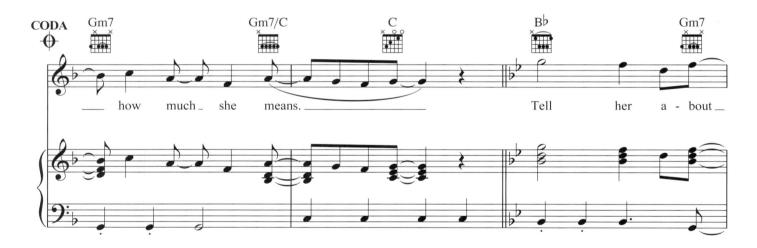

UPTOWN GIRL

Words and Music by
BILLY JOEL

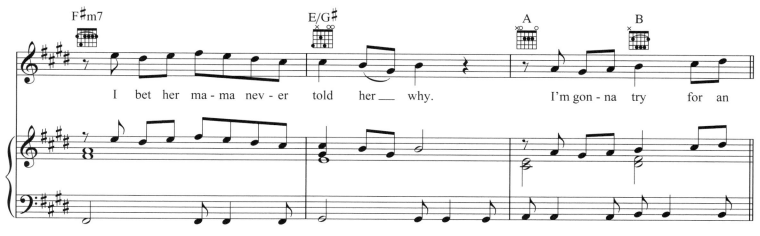

I bet her ma - ma nev - er told her ___ why. I'm gon - na try for an

up - town girl. She's been liv - ing in her white bread ___ world
Up - town girl, you know I can't af - ford to buy her ___ pearls.

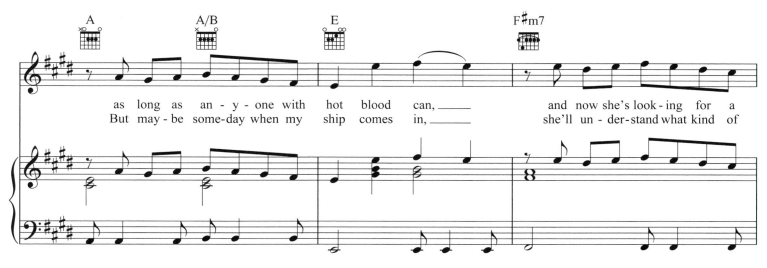

as long as an - y - one with hot blood can, ___ and now she's look - ing for a
But may - be some - day when my ship comes in, ___ she'll un - der - stand what kind of

down - town ___ man; that's what I am. And when she
guy I've ___ been and then I'll win. And when she's

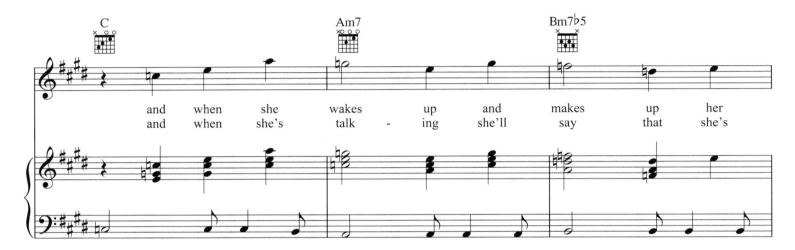

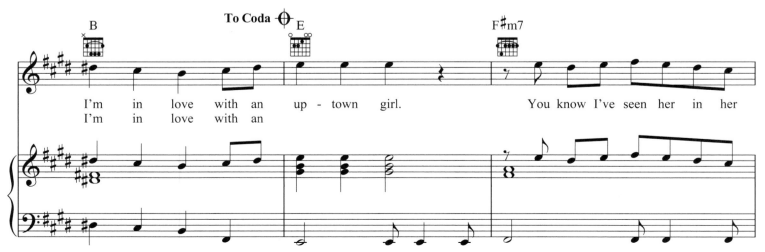

up - town __ world. She's get - ting tired __ of her high-class toys _____

and all her pres - ents from her up - town __ boys. She's got a choice.

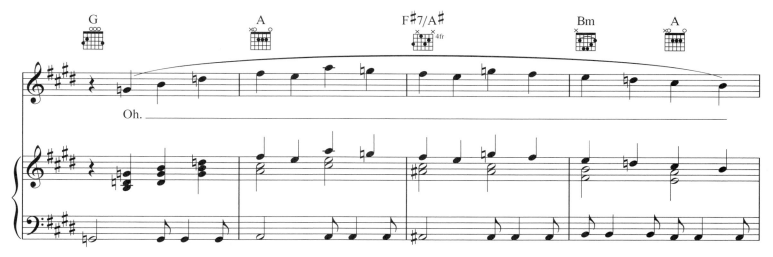

Oh. _____

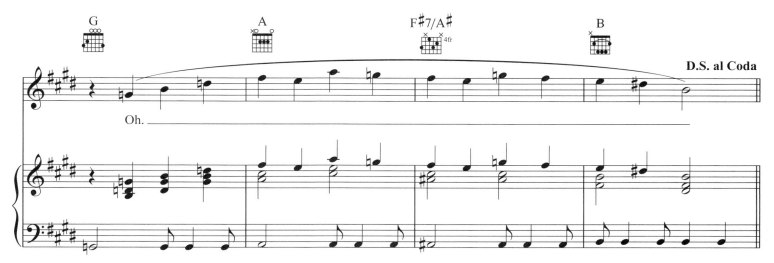

Oh. _____

D.S. al Coda

CODA

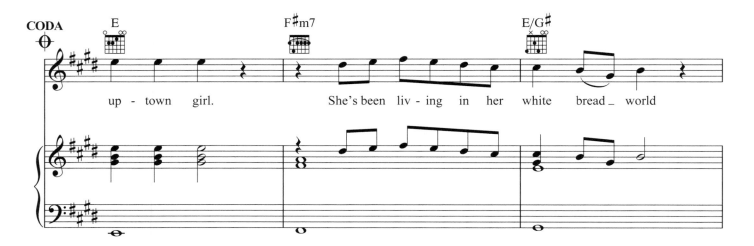

up - town girl. She's been liv - ing in her white bread _ world

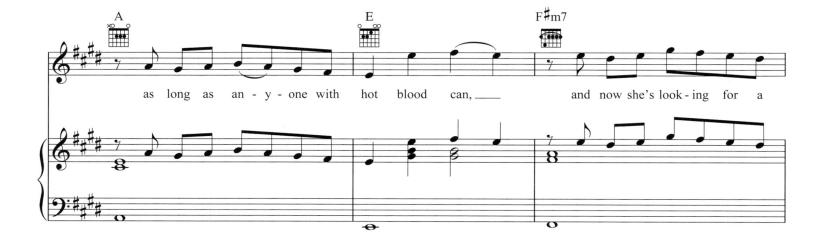

as long as an - y - one with hot blood can, _ and now she's look - ing for a

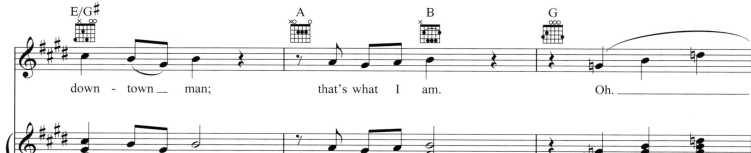

down - town _ man; that's what I am. Oh. _

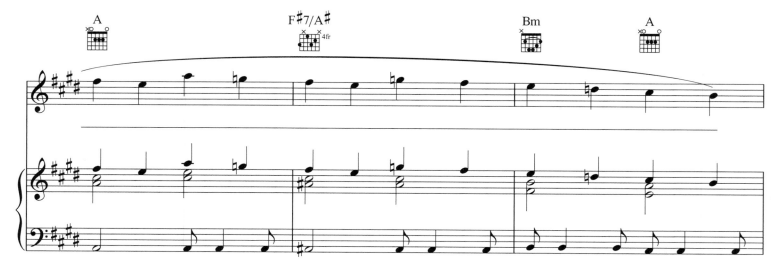

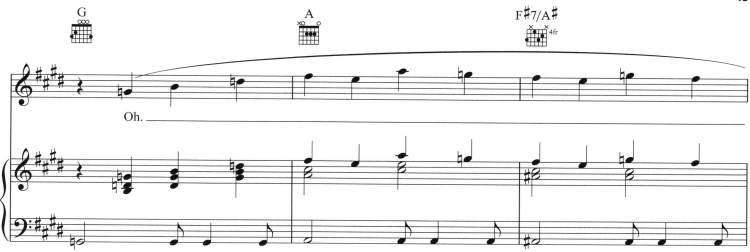

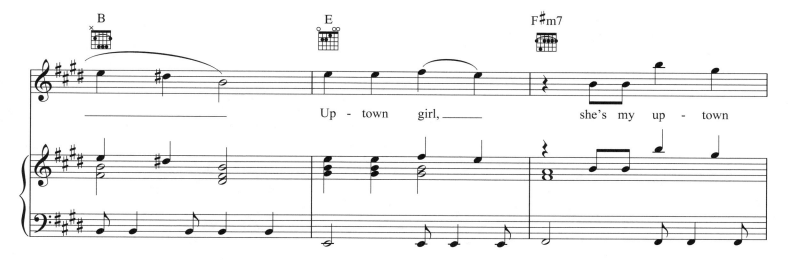

CARELESS TALK

Words and Music by
BILLY JOEL

Moderate Rock and Roll

Oh. _____ Oh. _____

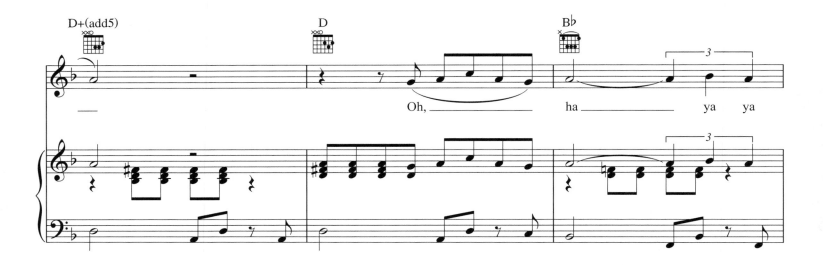

Oh, _____ ha _____ ya ya

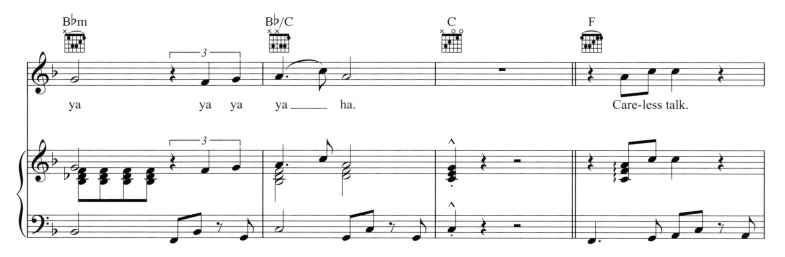

ya   ya ya ya _____ ha.   Care-less talk.

That's what you heard a-bout me.

Jeal-ous talk. That's what I heard a-bout you.

Ev-'ry-bod-y's tell-ing lies.

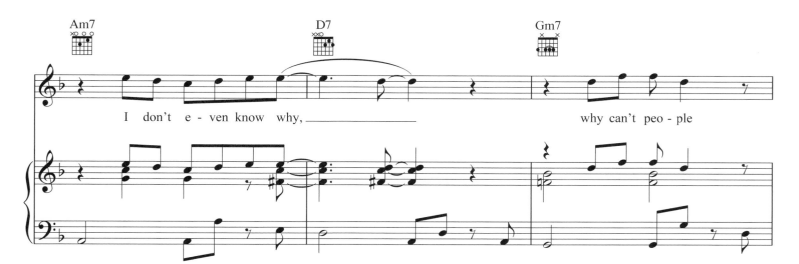

I don't e-ven know why, why can't peo-ple

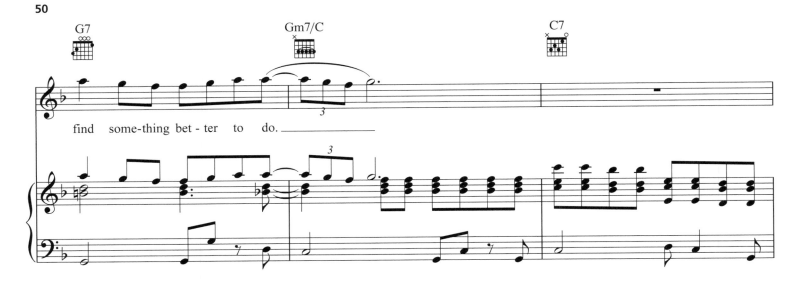

find some-thing bet-ter to do. _____

Care-less talk. I don't be-lieve _ what they say. ____
Care-less talk. Go - ing a - round _ on the streets. _

I heard them talk; they say you've been put - ting me down. _
Jeal - ous talk. I know how bad _ it can be. ___

In the shad - ows, on the
Let them stand where they _

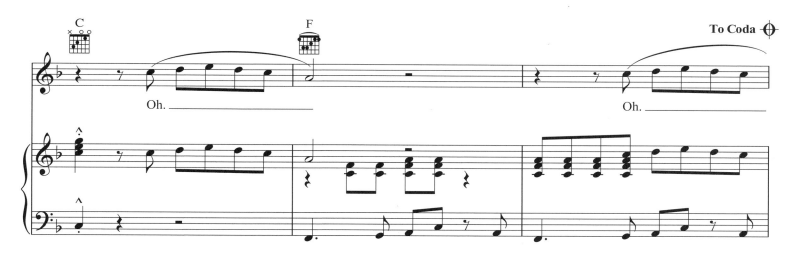

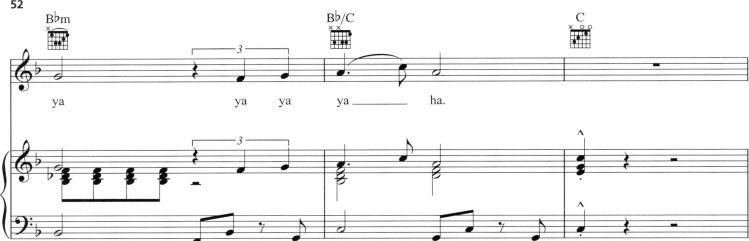

Care-less talk tell-ing you I'm ___ do-ing wrong. ___

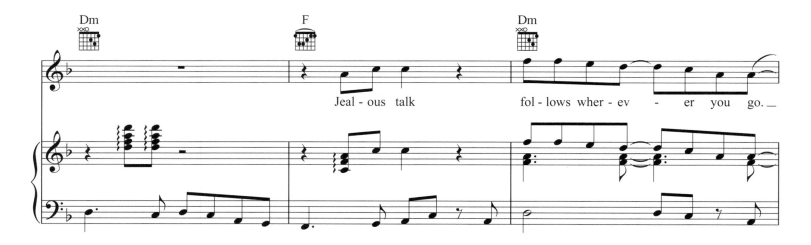

Jeal-ous talk fol-lows wher-ev - er you go. ___

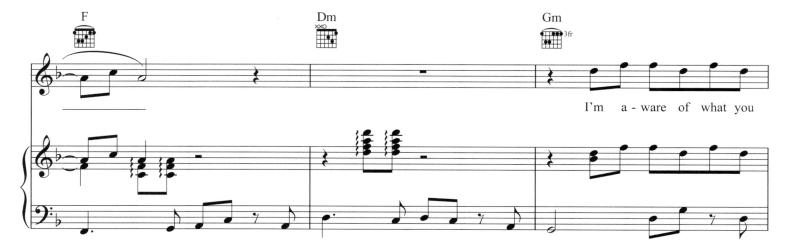

I'm a-ware of what you

heard. _____ Ev - 'ry ter - ri - ble word. _____

Ev - 'ry - bod - y's mak - ing be - lieve __ that they know _____

all of the in - ti - mate things ___ that we ev - er might __ have said ___

___ in the heat of a pas - sion - ate mo - ment, in a con -

54

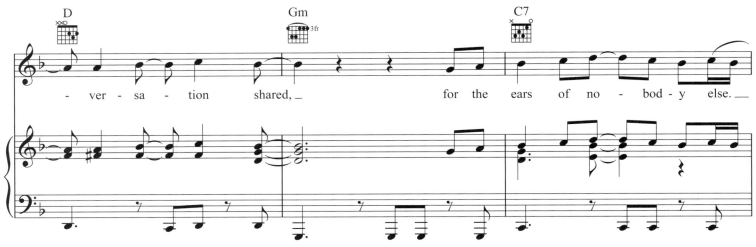

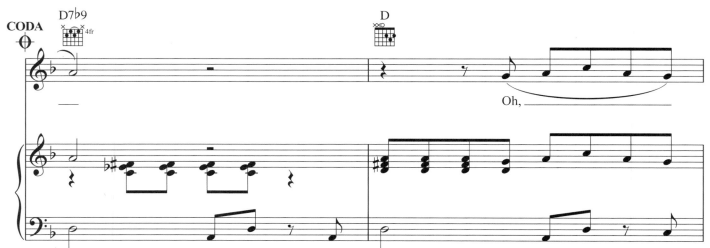

ha _____ ya ya ya _____ ya ya ya _____ ha.

Oh. _____ Care-less talk. That's what they say ___ a-bout me. _

Care-less talk.
Care-less talk.

Repeat and Fade

That's what they say ___ a-bout you. ___
That's what they say a-bout me. _____

CHRISTIE LEE

Words and Music by
BILLY JOEL

Chris-tie Lee, Chris-tie Lee.

Chris-tie Lee, Chris-tie

Lee.

Ooo

ooo.

D.S. al Coda

She was a nice piece of

CODA

al - to

and took it home with Chris-tie Lee.

Oh, _____ I heard the man knew "the Bird" like the Bi - ble, you know the

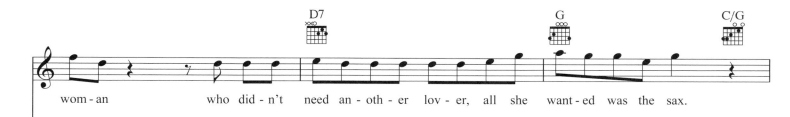

man could blow an ed - u - cat - ed axe. He could-n't see that Chris-tie Lee was a

wom - an who did -n't need an - oth - er lov - er, all she want - ed was the sax.

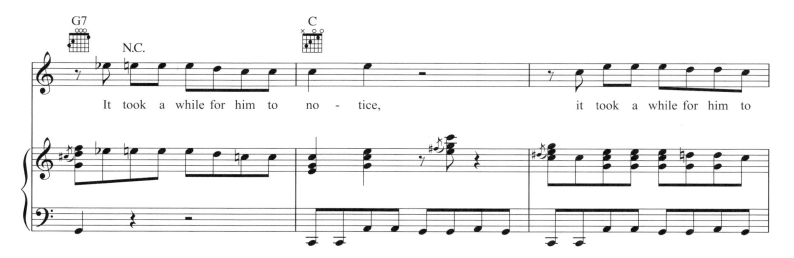

It took a while for him to no - tice, it took a while for him to

62

LEAVE A TENDER MOMENT ALONE

Words and Music by
BILLY JOEL

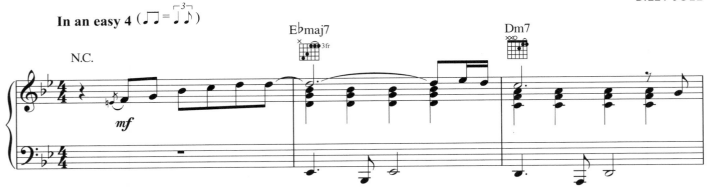

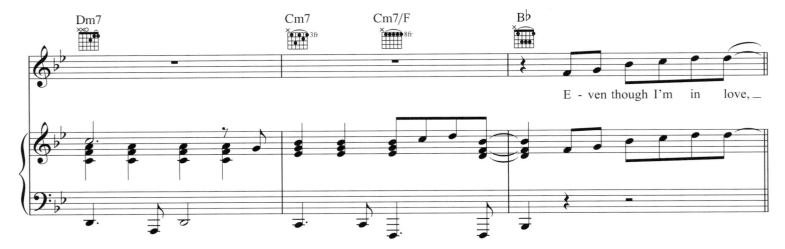

E - ven though I'm in love, __

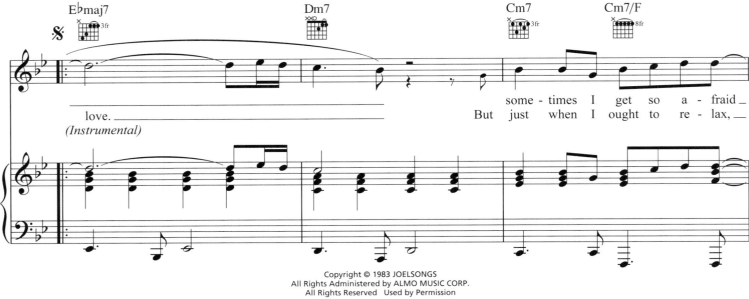

love. __
(Instrumental)

some - times I get so a - fraid __
But just when I ought to re - lax, __

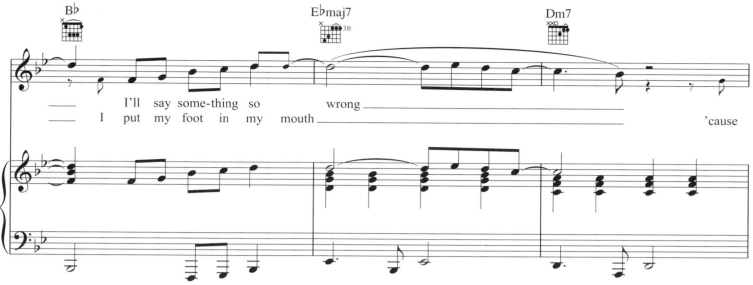

I'll say some-thing so wrong _____
I put my foot in my mouth _____ 'cause

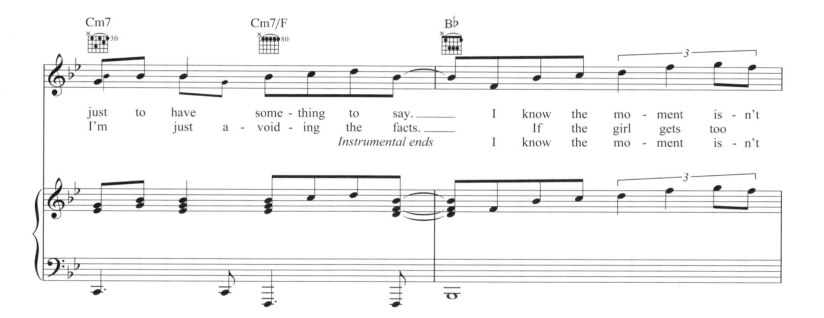

just to have some-thing to say. _____ I know the mo-ment is-n't
I'm just a-void-ing the facts. _____ If the girl gets too
Instrumental ends I know the mo-ment is-n't

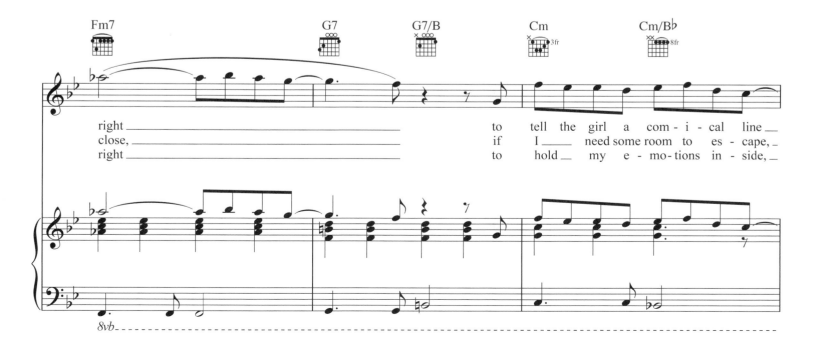

right _____ to tell the girl a com-i-cal line __
close, _____ if I _____ need some room to es-cape, __
right _____ to hold __ my e-mo-tions in-side, __

8vb -

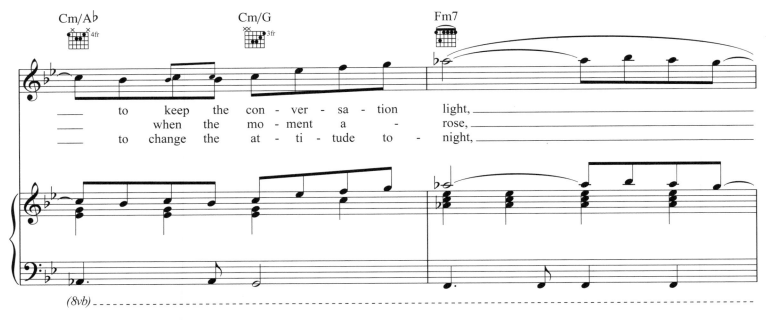

_to keep the con - ver - sa - tion light, _____
when the mo - ment a - rose, _____
to change the at - ti - tude to - night, _____

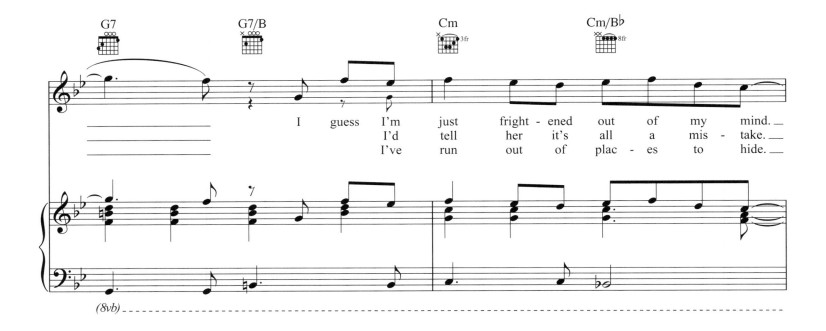

I guess I'm just fright - ened out of my mind. __
I'd just tell her it's all a mis - take. __
I've run out of plac - es to hide. __

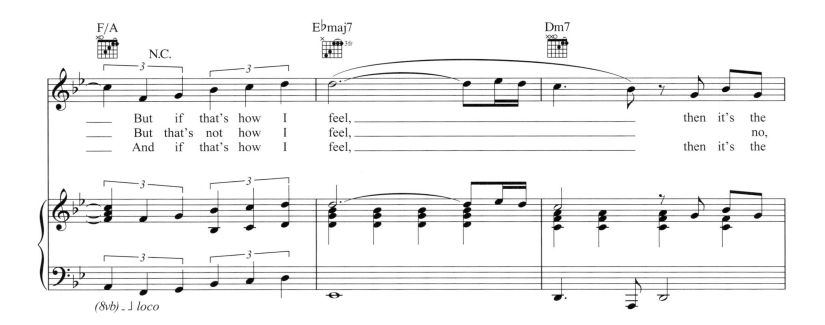

___ But if that's how I feel, _____ then it's the
___ But that's not how I feel, _____ no,
___ And if that's how I feel, _____ then it's the

68

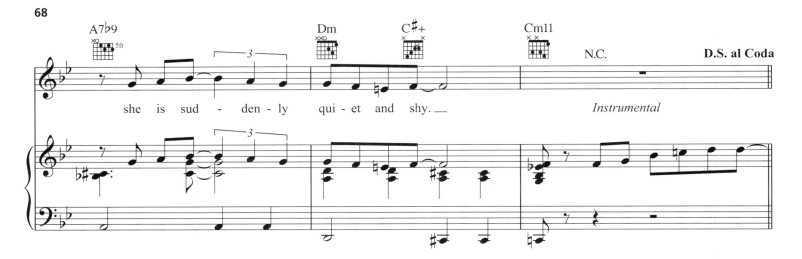

she is sud - den - ly qui - et and shy. ___   *Instrumental*

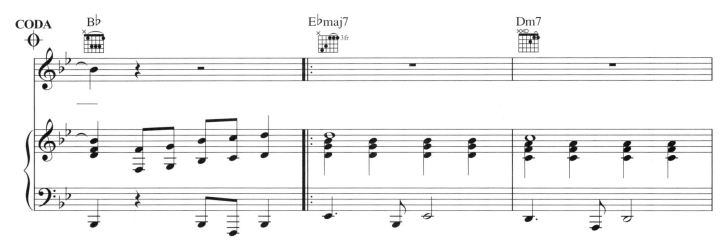

Leave a ten - der mo - ment a - lone. ___

Leave a ten - der mo - ment a - lone. ___

KEEPING THE FAITH

Words and Music by
BILLY JOEL

If it

seems like I've been lost in let's re - mem - ber,   if you

think I'm feel-ing old - er and miss-ing my young - er days, _____   oh, _____ then you

should have known＿ me much bet - ter, 'cause my past is some - thing that nev - er got in my

way, oh no. ＿ Still I

would not be here now if I nev - er had the hun - ger, and I'm

not a - shamed＿ to say the wild boys were my friends. ＿ Oh ＿ 'cause I

never felt _ the de - sire _____ 'til their mu - sic set _ me on fire, _ then I was

saved, yeah. _ That's why I'm keep - ing the faith. _

_ Yeah, yeah, _ yeah, _ yeah keep - ing the faith. _

_ We wore

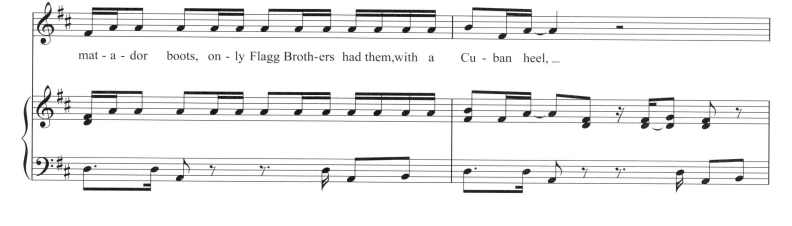

mat - a - dor boots, on - ly Flagg Broth-ers had them, with a Cu - ban heel, _

Ir - i - des-cent socks with the same col - or shirt, and a tight pair of chi - nos. _ Oh, I

put on my shark-skin jack- et, you know the kind with the vel - vet col - lar and dit - ty-bop

shades, oh yeah. _ I took a

fresh pack of Luck-ies and a mint called Sen - Sen, my

old man's Tro-jans and his Old Spice af - ter - shave. _____ Oh, _____ combed my

G

hair in a pom - pa - dour ___ like the rest of the Ro - me - os wore, a per - ma - nent

D/A   G/B   F#m/A

wave,   yeah. _   We were keep-ing the faith. ___

Yeah, yeah, yeah, yeah, keep-ing the faith.

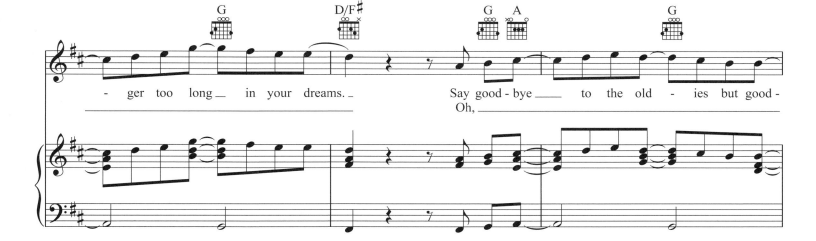

You can get just so much from a good thing, you can lin-
Oh _____ Oh _____

- ger too long in your dreams. Say good-bye to the old -ies but good-
Oh, _____

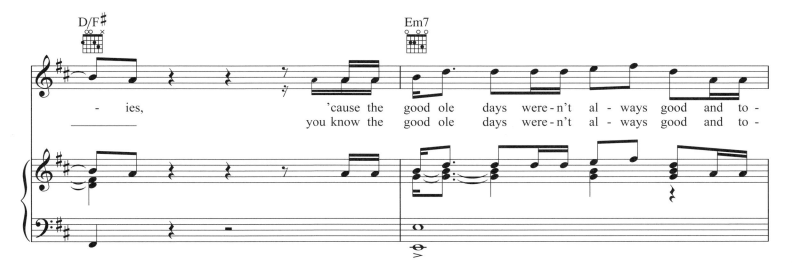

- ies, 'cause the good ole days were-n't al-ways good and to-
you know the good ole days were-n't al-ways good and to-

did.___ I found out a man ain't just be - ing ma - cho,

ate an aw - ful lot of late night drive - in food,

drank a lot of take - home pay.___ I thought I was the Duke of Earl _ when I

G

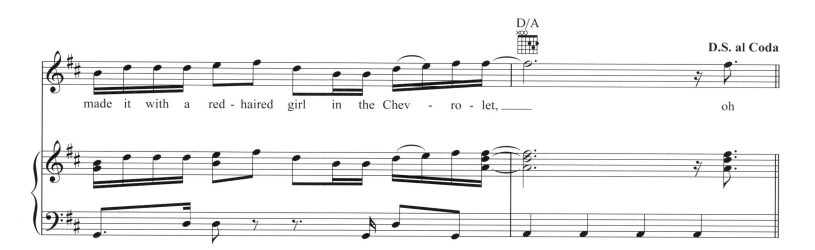

D/A

D.S. al Coda

made it with a red - haired girl in the Chev - ro - let,___ oh

won-der-ful to be a - live __ when the rock and roll plays,

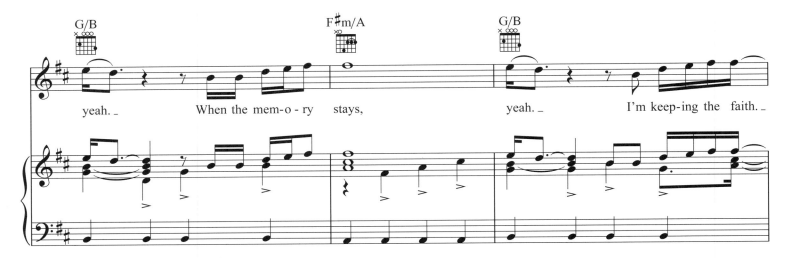

yeah. __   When the mem-o - ry stays,   yeah. __   I'm keep-ing the faith. __

Yeah, yeah, __ yeah, __ yeah keep-ing the faith. __

I'm keep-ing the faith, __   yes, I

am you know I'm keep-ing the faith. ___

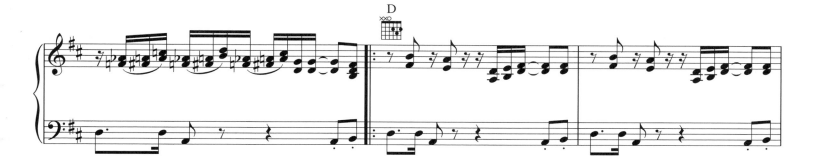

Repeat and Fade

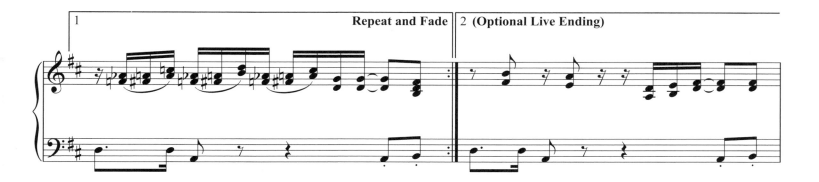